This booklet provides a general overview of basic topics related to OSHA and how it operates. Information provided does not determine compliance responsibilities under OSHA standards or the *Occupational Safety and Health Act of 1970* (OSH Act).

Because interpretations and enforcement policy may change over time, you should consult the agency for the most up-to-date information. Much of it is available at the OSHA website at www.osha.gov. The website also includes locations and phone numbers for OSHA offices around the country. If you do not have access to the website, call 1-800-321-OSHA (6742). This information is available to sensory-impaired individuals upon request. Voice phone: (202) 693-1999; teletypewriter (TTY) number: (877) 889-5627.

Cover photo: Steve Baranowski, Braintree, Massachusetts Area Office

All About **OSHA**

U.S. Department of Labor

Occupational Safety and Health Administration

OSHA 3302-09R
2014

U.S. Department of Labor

OSHA®

Contents

OSHA

A Message from Dr. David Michaels

In 1970, the United States Congress and President Richard Nixon created the Occupational Safety and Health Administration (OSHA), a national public health agency dedicated to the basic proposition that no worker should have to choose between their life and their job.

Passed with bipartisan support, the creation of OSHA was a historic moment of cooperative national reform. The OSHA law makes it clear that the right to a safe workplace is a basic human right.

Since OSHA's first day on the job, the agency has delivered remarkable progress for our nation. Workplace injuries, illnesses and deaths have fallen dramatically. Together with our state partners, OSHA has tackled deadly safety hazards and health risks. We have established common sense standards and enforced the law against those who put workers at risk. Our standards, enforcement actions, compliance assistance and cooperative programs have saved thousands of lives and prevented countless injuries and illnesses.

Looking to the future, OSHA is committed to protecting workers from toxic chemicals and deadly safety hazards at work, ensuring that vulnerable workers in high-risk jobs have access to critical information and education about job hazards, and providing employers with vigorous compliance assistance to promote best practices that can save lives.

Although our task is far from complete, our progress gives us hope and confidence that OSHA will continue to make a lasting difference in the lives of our nation's 130 million workers, their families and their communities.

David Michaels, PhD, MPH
Assistant Secretary of Labor for OSHA

OSHA®

OSHA's Mission

Congress created OSHA to assure safe and healthful conditions for working men and women by setting and enforcing standards and providing training, outreach, education and compliance assistance.

Under the OSHA law, employers are responsible for providing a safe and healthful workplace for their workers. For more information, visit OSHA's website at www.osha.gov.

Introduction

On December 29, 1970, President Nixon signed the *Occupational Safety and Health Act of 1970* (OSH Act) into law, establishing OSHA. Coupled with the efforts of employers, workers, safety and health professionals, unions and advocates, OSHA and its state partners have dramatically improved workplace safety, reducing work-related deaths and injuries by more than 65 percent.

Photo: James Majors

In 1970, an estimated 14,000 workers were killed on the job – about 38 every day. For 2010, the Bureau of Labor Statistics reports this number fell to about 4,500 or about 12 workers per day. At the same time, U.S. employment has almost doubled to over 130 million workers at more than 7.2 million worksites. The rate of reported serious workplace injuries and illnesses has also dropped markedly, from 11 per 100 workers in 1972 to 3.5 per 100 workers in 2010.

OSHA's safety and health standards, including those for asbestos, fall protection, cotton dust, trenching, machine guarding, benzene, lead and bloodborne pathogens have prevented countless work-related injuries, illnesses and deaths. Nevertheless, far too many preventable injuries and fatalities continue to occur. Significant hazards and unsafe conditions still exist in U.S. workplaces; each year more than 3.3 million working men and women suffer a serious job-related injury or illness. Millions more are exposed to toxic chemicals that may cause illnesses years from now.

In addition to the direct impact on individual workers, the negative consequences for America's economy are substantial. Occupational injuries and illnesses cost American employers more than $53 billion a year – over $1 billion a week – in workers' compensation costs alone. Indirect costs to employers, including lost productivity, employee training and replacement costs, and time for investigations following injuries can more than double these costs. Workers and their families suffer great emotional and psychological costs, in addition to the loss of wages and the costs of caring for the injured, which further weakens the economy.

OSHA Coverage

The OSH Act covers most private sector employers and their workers, in addition to some public sector employers and workers in the 50 states and certain territories and jurisdictions under federal authority. Those jurisdictions include the District of Columbia, Puerto Rico, the Virgin Islands, American Samoa, Guam, Northern Mariana Islands, Wake Island, Johnston Island, and the Outer Continental Shelf Lands as defined in the *Outer Continental Shelf Lands Act*.

Private Sector Workers

OSHA covers most private sector employers and workers in all 50 states, the District of Columbia, and other U.S., jurisdictions either directly through Federal OSHA or through an OSHA-approved state plan.

State plans are OSHA-approved job safety and health programs operated by individual states instead of Federal OSHA. The OSH Act encourages states to develop and operate their own job safety and health programs and precludes state enforcement of OSHA standards unless the state has an approved program. OSHA approves and monitors all state plans and provides as much as fifty percent of the funding for each program. State-run safety and health programs must be at least as effective as the Federal OSHA program. To find the contact information for the OSHA Federal or state plan office nearest you, call 1-800-321-OSHA (6742) or go to www.osha.gov.

The following 22 states or territories have OSHA-approved state programs:

- Alaska
- Arizona
- California
- Hawaii
- Indiana
- Iowa
- Kentucky
- Maryland
- Michigan
- Minnesota
- Nevada
- New Mexico
- North Carolina
- Oregon
- Puerto Rico
- South Carolina
- Tennessee
- Utah

OSHA

OSHA-Approved State Plans

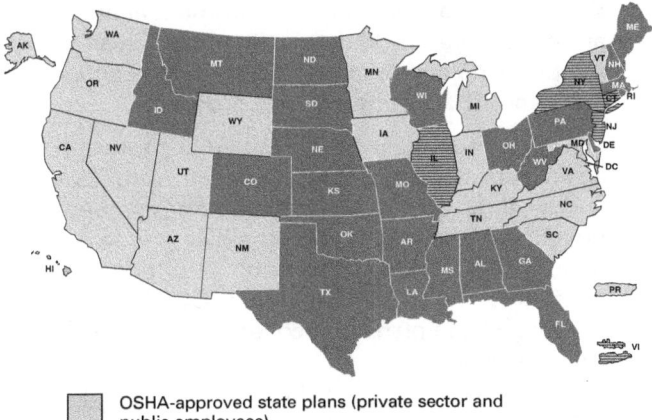

☐ OSHA-approved state plans (private sector and public employees)

■ Federal OSHA (private sector and most federal employees)

▤ OSHA-approved state plans (for public employees only; private sector employees are covered by Federal OSHA)

- Vermont
- Washington
- Virginia
- Wyoming

Federal OSHA provides coverage to certain workers specifically excluded from a state's plan, for example, those in some states who work in maritime industries or on military bases.

Any interested person or group, including individual workers, with a complaint concerning the operation or administration of a state program may submit a complaint to the appropriate Federal OSHA regional administrator (regional offices are listed at the end of this guide). This is called a Complaint About State Program Administration (CASPA). The complainant's name will be kept confidential. The OSHA regional administrator will investigate all such complaints, and where complaints are found to be valid, may require appropriate corrective action on the part of the state.

State and Local Government Workers

Workers at state and local government agencies are not covered by Federal OSHA, but have OSH Act protections if they work in those states that have an OSHA-approved state program.

OSHA rules also permit states and territories to develop plans that cover only public sector (state and local government) workers. In these cases, private sector workers and employers remain under Federal OSHA jurisdiction. Four additional states and one U.S. territory have OSHA-approved state plans that cover public sector workers only:

- Connecticut
- Illinois
- New Jersey
- New York
- Virgin Islands

Federal Government Workers

OSHA's protection applies to all federal agencies. Section 19 of the OSH Act makes federal agency heads responsible for providing safe and healthful working conditions for their workers. Although OSHA does not fine federal agencies, it does monitor these agencies and conducts federal workplace inspections in response to workers' reports of hazards.

Federal agencies must have a safety and health program that meets the same standards as private employers. Under a 1998 amendment, the OSH Act covers the U.S. Postal Service the same as any private sector employer.

Not Covered under the OSH Act

- The self-employed;
- Immediate family members of farm employers; and
- Workplace hazards regulated by another federal agency (for example, the Mine Safety and Health Administration, the Department of Energy, or Coast Guard).

OSHA

Rights and Responsibilities under OSHA Law

Employers have the responsibility to provide a safe workplace. **Employers MUST provide their workers with a workplace that does not have serious hazards and must follow all OSHA safety and health standards.** Employers must find and correct safety and health problems. OSHA further requires that employers must first try to eliminate or reduce hazards by making feasible changes in working conditions rather than relying on personal protective equipment such as masks, gloves, or earplugs. Switching to safer chemicals, enclosing processes to trap harmful fumes, or using ventilation systems to clean the air are examples of effective ways to eliminate or reduce risks.

Employers MUST also:

- Prominently display the official OSHA *Job Safety and Health – It's the Law* poster that describes rights and responsibilities under the OSH Act. **This poster is free and can be downloaded from www.osha.gov.**
- Inform workers about chemical hazards through training, labels, alarms, color-coded systems, chemical information sheets and other methods.
- Provide safety training to workers in a language and vocabulary they can understand.
- Keep accurate records of work-related injuries and illnesses.
- Perform tests in the workplace, such as air sampling, required by some OSHA standards.
- Provide required personal protective equipment at no cost to workers.*
- Provide hearing exams or other medical tests required by OSHA standards.
- Post OSHA citations and injury and illness data where workers can see them.

OSHA®

- As of January 1, 2015, notify OSHA within 8 hours of a workplace fatality or within 24 hours of any work-related inpatient hospitalization, amputation or loss of an eye (1-800-321-OSHA [6742]).
- Not retaliate against workers for using their rights under the law, including their right to report a work-related injury or illness.

* Employers must pay for most types of required personal protective equipment.

Workers have the right to:
- Working conditions that do not pose a risk of serious harm.
- File a confidential complaint with OSHA to have their workplace inspected.
- Receive information and training about hazards, methods to prevent harm, and the OSHA standards that apply to their workplace. The training must be done in a language and vocabulary workers can understand.
- Receive copies of records of work-related injuries and illnesses that occur in their workplace.
- Receive copies of the results from tests and monitoring done to find and measure hazards in their workplace.
- Receive copies of their workplace medical records.
- Participate in an OSHA inspection and speak in private with the inspector.
- File a complaint with OSHA if they have been retaliated against by their employer as the result of requesting an inspection or using any of their other rights under the OSH Act.
- File a complaint if punished or retaliated against for acting as a "whistleblower" under the 21 additional federal laws for which OSHA has jurisdiction.

OSHA Standards

OSHA's Construction, General Industry, Maritime and Agriculture standards protect workers from a wide range of serious hazards. Examples of OSHA standards include requirements for employers to:

- provide fall protection;
- prevent trenching cave-ins;
- prevent exposure to some infectious diseases;
- ensure the safety of workers who enter confined spaces;
- prevent exposure to harmful chemicals;
- put guards on dangerous machines;
- provide respirators or other safety equipment; and
- provide training for certain dangerous jobs in a language and vocabulary workers can understand.

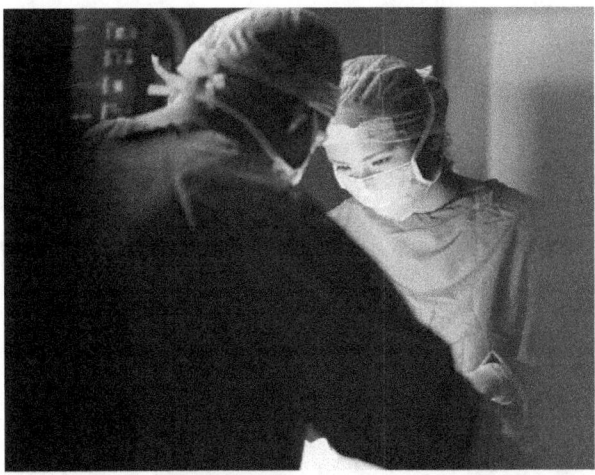

Employers must also comply with the General Duty Clause of the OSH Act. This clause requires employers to keep their workplaces free of serious recognized hazards and is generally cited when no specific OSHA standard applies to the hazard.

The Standards-Setting Process

OSHA has the authority to issue new or revised occupational safety and health standards. The OSHA standards-setting process involves many steps and provides many opportunities for public engagement. OSHA can begin standards-setting procedures on its own initiative or in response to recommendations or petitions from other parties, including:

- The National Institute for Occupational Safety and Health (NIOSH), the research agency for occupational safety and health. (For more information, call 1-800-CDC-INFO (1-800-232-4636) or visit the agency's website at www.cdc.gov/niosh);
- State and local governments;
- Nationally recognized standards-producing organizations;
- Employer or labor representatives; and
- Any other interested parties.

When OSHA is considering whether to develop a new or revised standard, the Agency often publishes a Request for Information (RFI) or an Advance Notice of Proposed Rulemaking

(ANPRM) in the Federal Register to obtain information and views from interested members of the public. OSHA will also frequently hold stakeholder meetings with interested parties to solicit information and opinions on how the Agency should proceed with the regulation. When OSHA publishes an RFI or ANPRM, interested parties can submit written comments at www. regulations.gov, where all information and submissions are made public.

If OSHA decides to proceed with issuing a new or revised regulation, it must first publish a Notice of Proposed Rulemaking (NPRM) in the Federal Register and solicit public comment. The NPRM contains a proposed standard along with OSHA's explanation of the need for the various requirements in that proposed standard.

Interested parties are invited to submit written comments through www.regulations.gov, and OSHA will often hold public hearings in which stakeholders can offer testimony and provide information to assist the Agency in developing a final standard. After considering all of the information and testimony provided, OSHA develops and issues a final standard that becomes enforceable.

Each spring and fall, the Department of Labor publishes in the Federal Register a list of all regulatory projects underway. The Regulatory Agenda provides a projected schedule for these projects to inform stakeholders of the Agency's regulatory priorities and enable interested parties to take advantage of opportunities to participate in the regulatory process. Current and past issues of the Regulatory Agenda can be accessed on OSHA's Law and Regulations page at www.osha. gov/law-regs.html.

Input from Small Business

The *Small Business Regulatory Enforcement Fairness Act of 1996* (SBREFA) gives small businesses help in understanding and complying with OSHA regulations and allows them a voice in developing new regulations. Under SBREFA, OSHA must:

- Produce Small Entity Compliance Guides for some agency rules;
- Be responsive to small business inquiries about complying with the Agency's regulations;
- Have a penalty reduction policy for small businesses;
- Involve small businesses in developing proposed rules expected to significantly affect a large number of small entities through Small Business Advocacy Review Panels; and
- Give small businesses the opportunity to challenge in court agency rules or regulations that they believe will adversely affect them.

More information about OSHA standards and the standards-setting process is available on OSHA's website at www.osha.gov. Standards can be viewed on OSHA's Law and Regulations page at www.osha.gov/law-regs.html.

Enforcement

OSHA Inspection Activities: Carrying Out Our Mission

Enforcement plays an important part in OSHA's efforts to reduce workplace injuries, illnesses, and fatalities. When OSHA finds employers who fail to uphold their safety and health responsibilities, the agency takes strong, decisive actions.

Inspections are initiated without advance notice, conducted using on-site or telephone and facsimile investigations, performed by highly trained compliance officers and scheduled based on the following priorities:

- Imminent danger;
- Catastrophes – fatalities or hospitalizations;

OSHA

- Worker complaints and referrals;
- Targeted inspections – particular hazards, high injury rates; and
- Follow-up inspections.

Current workers or their representatives may file a written complaint and ask OSHA to inspect their workplace if they believe there is a serious hazard or that their employer is not following OSHA standards. Workers and their representatives have the right to ask for an inspection without OSHA telling their employer who filed the complaint. It is a violation of the OSH Act for an employer to fire, demote, transfer or in any way retaliate against a worker for filing a complaint or using other OSHA rights.

Photo: Aaron Sussell, Cincinnati, Ohio

The on-site inspection begins with the presentation of the compliance officer's credentials. The compliance officer will explain why OSHA selected the workplace for inspection and describe the scope of the inspection process, walkaround procedures, employee representation and employee interviews. Following the opening conference, the compliance officer and the representatives will walk through portions of the workplace covered by the inspection, inspecting for hazards that could lead to worker injury or illness. After the walkaround, the compliance officer will hold a closing conference with the employer and the employee representative to discuss the findings.

When an inspector finds violations of OSHA standards or serious hazards, OSHA may issue citations and fines. A citation includes methods an employer may use to fix a problem and the date by which the corrective actions must be completed.

Employers have the right to contest any part of the citation, including whether a violation actually exists. Workers only have the right to challenge the deadline by which a problem must be resolved. Appeals of citations are heard by the independent Occupational Safety and Health Review Commission (OSHRC). To contact the OSHRC, visit www.oshrc.gov or call (202) 606-5370.

OSHA carries out its enforcement activities through its 10 regional offices and 90 area offices. OSHA's regional offices are located in Boston, New York City, Philadelphia, Atlanta, Chicago, Dallas, Kansas City, Denver, San Francisco and Seattle. Contact information for each regional office is available at the end of this guide.

Severe Violator Enforcement Program

OSHA's Severe Violator Enforcement Program (SVEP) became effective on June 18, 2010. The program focuses enforcement efforts on employers who willfully and repeatedly endanger workers by exposing them to serious hazards. The SVEP directive establishes procedures and enforcement actions for these violators, including mandatory follow-up inspections of workplaces found in violation and inspections of other worksites of the same company where similar hazards or deficiencies may be present. Visit www.osha.gov for more information.

General Reporting and
Recordkeeping Requirements

OSHA's Reporting Requirements

As of January 1, 2015, all employers must report
to OSHA:

- The death of any worker from a work-related
  incident within 8 hours of learning about it;
- All work-related inpatient hospitalizations,
  amputations and losses of an eye within
  24 hours.

For more information, visit www.osha.gov/
recordkeeping2014.

In addition, employers must report all fatal heart
attacks that occur at work. Deaths from motor
vehicle accidents on public streets (except those
in a construction work zone) and in accidents on
commercial airplanes, trains, subways or buses
do not need to be reported.

These reports may be made by telephone or in
person to the nearest OSHA area office listed
at www.osha.gov or by calling OSHA's toll-free
number, 1-800-321-OSHA (6742).

OSHA's Recordkeeping Requirements

Tracking and investigating workplace injuries and
illnesses play an important role in preventing
future injuries and illnesses, and for that reason,
OSHA requires certain covered employers in high-
hazard industries to prepare and maintain records
of serious work-related injuries and illnesses.

Employers with more than ten employees and
whose establishments are not classified as a
partially exempt industry must record serious
work-related injuries and illnesses using OSHA
Forms 300, 300A and 301, which are available
at www.osha.gov/recordkeeping/RKforms.
html. A list of partially exempt industries,
including establishments in specific low hazard
retail, service, finance, insurance or real estate

industries is available at www.osha.gov/
recordkeeping/ppt1/RK1exempttable.html.
Employers who are required to keep Form 300,
the Injury and Illness log, must also post Form
300A, the Summary of Work-Related Injuries
and Illnesses, in the workplace every year from
February 1 to April 30. For more information, visit
www.osha.gov/recordkeeping.

Employers and workers need accurate, timely
information to focus their prevention activities,
and OSHA uses this information for many
purposes, including inspection targeting,
performance measurement, standards
development and resource allocation. Injury and
illness data also aid employers and workers in
identifying possible safety and health hazards at
the employer's establishment. OSHA encourages
employers to review and investigate patterns
of injuries and illnesses, and to conduct
investigations of injuries and near misses to
prevent similar events in the future.

OSHA is responsible for administering the
recordkeeping system established by the OSH
Act. OSHA's recordkeeping regulations provide
specific recording and reporting requirements
which comprise the framework for the nationwide
occupational safety and health recordkeeping
system. For more information about OSHA's
recordkeeping requirements visit www.osha.gov/
recordkeeping.

Filing a Complaint
Hazardous Workplace Complaints
If a workplace has unsafe or unhealthful working
conditions, workers may want to file a complaint.
Often the best and fastest way to get a hazard
corrected is to notify a supervisor or employer.

OSHA®

Workers or their representatives may file a complaint online or by phone, mail, email or fax with the nearest OSHA office and request an inspection. A worker may also ask OSHA not to reveal his or her name. To file a complaint, call 1-800-321-OSHA (6742) or contact the nearest OSHA regional, area, state plan, or consultation office listed at www.osha.gov. The teletypewriter (TTY) number is (877) 889-5627.

Written, signed complaints submitted to OSHA area offices are more likely to result in an on-site OSHA inspection. Most online or unsigned complaints are resolved informally over the phone with the employer. Complaints from workers in states with an OSHA-approved state plan will be forwarded to the appropriate state plan for response.

Workers can call 1-800-321-OSHA (6742) to request a complaint form from their local OSHA office or visit www.osha.gov/pls/osha7/eComplaintForm.html to submit the form online. Completed forms can also be faxed or mailed to the local OSHA office (provided at the end of this guide). Include your name, address and telephone number so that OSHA can contact you.

OSHA's Whistleblower Program: Protection from Retaliation

To help ensure that workers are free to participate in safety and health activities, Section 11(c) of the OSH Act prohibits any person from discharging or in any manner retaliating against any worker for exercising rights under the OSH Act. These rights include raising safety and health concerns with an employer, reporting a work-related injury or illness, filing a complaint with OSHA, seeking an OSHA inspection, participating in an OSHA inspection and participating or testifying in any proceeding related to an OSHA inspection.

Protection from retaliation means that an employer cannot retaliate by taking "adverse action" against workers, such as:

- Firing or laying off;
- Blacklisting;
- Demoting;
- Denying overtime or promotion;
- Disciplining;
- Denying of benefits;
- Failing to hire or rehire;
- Intimidation;
- Making threats;
- Reassignment affecting prospects for promotion; or
- Reducing pay or hours.

If a worker believes an employer has retaliated against them for exercising their safety and health rights, they should contact their local OSHA office right away. You must file a retaliation complaint with OSHA within 30 calendar days from the date the retaliatory decision has been both made and communicated to the worker. **No form is needed, but workers must call OSHA within 30 days of the alleged retaliation** (at 1-800-321-OSHA [6742]). For more information, please visit www.whistleblowers.gov.

If There is a Dangerous Situation at Work

If a worker believes working conditions are unsafe or unhealthful, OSHA recommends that he or she bring the conditions to the employer's attention, if possible. A worker may file a complaint with OSHA concerning a hazardous working condition at any time. However, workers should not leave the worksite merely because they have filed a complaint. If the condition clearly presents a risk of death or serious physical harm, there is not sufficient time for OSHA to inspect, and, where possible, a worker has brought the condition to the attention of the

OSHA

Photo: Frank Wenzel, Washington DOSH

employer, the worker may have a legal right to refuse to work in a situation in which he or she would be exposed to the hazard.

If a worker, with no reasonable alternative, refuses in good faith to expose himself or herself to a dangerous condition, he or she would be protected from subsequent retaliation. The condition must be of such a nature that a reasonable person would conclude that there is a real danger of death or serious harm and that there is not enough time to contact OSHA and for OSHA to inspect. Where possible, the worker must have also sought from his or her employer, and been unable to obtain, a correction of the condition. For more information, go to www.osha.gov/workers.html.

Additional Whistleblower Protections
Since passage of the OSH Act in 1970, Congress has expanded OSHA's whistleblower protection authority to protect workers from retaliation under a total of 22 federal laws. These laws

protect workers who report violations of various workplace safety, airline, commercial motor carrier, consumer product, environmental, financial reform, healthcare reform, nuclear, pipeline, public transportation agency, railroad, maritime and securities laws. Complaints must be reported to OSHA within set timeframes following the retaliatory action, as prescribed by each law. These laws, and the number of days workers have to file a complaint, are:

Worker, Environmental and Nuclear Safety Laws

- *Asbestos Hazard Emergency Response Act (AHERA)* (90 days). Provides retaliation protection for individuals who report violations of environmental laws relating to asbestos in public or private nonprofit elementary and secondary school systems.
- *Clean Air Act (CAA)* (30 days). Provides retaliation protection for employees who, among other things, report violations of this law, which provides for the development and enforcement of standards regarding air quality and air pollution.
- *Comprehensive Environmental Response, Compensation, and Liability Act (CERCLA)* (30 days). Protects employees who report regulatory violations involving accidents, spills, and other emergency releases of pollutants into the environment. The law also protects employees who report violations related to the cleanup of uncontrolled or abandoned hazardous waste sites.
- *Energy Reorganization Act (ERA)* (180 days). Protects certain employees in the nuclear industry who report violations of the *Atomic Energy Act (AEA)*. Protected employees include employees of operators, contractors and subcontractors of nuclear power plants licensed by the Nuclear Regulatory Commission,

and employees of contractors working with the Department of Energy under a contract pursuant to the *Atomic Energy Act.*

- **Federal Water Pollution Control Act (FWPCA) (also known as the Clean Water Act)** (30 days). Provides retaliation protection for employees who, among other things, report violations of the law controlling water pollution.
- **Occupational Safety and Health Act of 1970** (30 days). Provides retaliation protection for employees who exercise a variety of rights guaranteed under this law, such as filing a safety and health complaint with OSHA and participating in an inspection.
- **Safe Drinking Water Act (SDWA)** (30 days). Provides retaliation protection for employees who, among other things, report violations of this law, which requires that all drinking water systems assure that their water is potable, as determined by the Environmental Protection Agency.
- **Solid Waste Disposal Act (SWDA) (also known as the Resource Conservation and Recovery Act)** (30 days). Provides retaliation protection for employees who, among other things, report violations of the law regulating the disposal of solid waste.
- **Toxic Substances Control Act (TSCA)** (30 days). Provides retaliation protection for employees who, among other things, report violations of regulations involving the manufacture, distribution, and use of certain toxic substances.

Transportation Industry Laws
- **Federal Railroad Safety Act (FRSA)** (180 days). Provides protection to employees of railroad carriers and contractors and subcontractors of those carriers who report an alleged violation of any federal law, rule, or regulation relating to railroad safety or security, or gross fraud,

OSHA

waste, or abuse of federal grants or other public funds intended to be used for railroad safety or security; report, in good faith, a hazardous safety or security condition; refuse to violate or assist in the violation of any federal law, rule, or regulation relating to railroad safety or security; refuse to work when confronted by a hazardous safety or security condition related to the performance of the employee's duties (under imminent danger circumstances); request prompt medical or first-aid treatment for employment-related injuries; are disciplined for requesting medical or first-aid treatment or for following an order or treatment plan of a treating physician.

- *International Safe Container Act (ISCA)* (60 days). Provides retaliation protection for employees who report violations of this law, which regulates shipping containers.
- *Moving Ahead for Progress in the 21st Century Act (MAP-21)* (180 days). Prohibits retaliation by motor vehicle manufacturers, part suppliers, and dealerships against employees for providing information to the employer or the U.S. Department of Transportation about motor vehicle defects, noncompliance, or violations of the notification or reporting requirements enforced by the National Highway Traffic Safety Administration or for engaging in related protected activities as set forth in the provision.
- *National Transit Systems Security Act (NTSSA)* (180 days). Provides protection to public transit employees who, among other things, report an alleged violation of any federal law, rule, or regulation relating to public transportation agency safety or security, or fraud, waste, or abuse of federal grants or other public funds intended to be used for public transportation safety or security; refuse to violate or assist in the violation of any federal law, rule, or regulation relating to public transportation safety or security; report a hazardous safety or security

condition; refuse to work when confronted by a hazardous safety or security condition related to the performance of the employee's duties (under imminent danger circumstances).

- **Pipeline Safety Improvement Act of 2002 (PSIA)** (180 days). Provides retaliation protection for employees who report violations of the federal laws regarding pipeline safety and security or who refuse to violate such provisions.
- **Seaman's Protection Act (SPA)** (180 days). Seamen are protected, among other things, for reporting to the Coast Guard or other federal agency a reasonably believed violation of a maritime safety law or regulation prescribed under that law or regulation. The law also protects work refusals where the employee reasonably believes an assigned task would result in serious injury or impairment of health to the seaman, other seamen, or the public and when the seaman sought, and was unable to obtain correction of the unsafe conditions.
- **Surface Transportation Assistance Act (STAA)** (180 days). Provides retaliation protection for truck drivers and other employees relating to the safety of commercial motor vehicles. Coverage includes all buses for hire and freight trucks with a gross vehicle weight greater than 10,001 pounds.
- **Wendell H. Ford Aviation Investment and Reform Act for the 21st Century (AIR21)** (90 days). Provides retaliation protection for employees of air carriers, contractors, or subcontractors of air carriers who, among other things, raise safety concerns.

Fraud Prevention Laws
- **Affordable Care Act (ACA)** (180 days). Protects employees who report violations of any provision of Title I of the ACA, including but not limited to retaliation based on an individual's receipt of health insurance

subsidies, the denial of coverage based on a preexisting condition, or an insurer's failure to rebate a portion of an excess premium.

- ***Consumer Financial Protection Act of 2010 (CFPA), Section 1057 of the Dodd-Frank Wall Street Reform and Consumer Protection Act*** (180 days). Protects employees who report perceived violations of any provision of the *Dodd-Frank Act,* which encompasses nearly every aspect of the financial services industry. The law also protects employees who report violations of any rule, order, standard or prohibition prescribed by the Bureau of Consumer Financial Protection.

- ***Section 806 of the Sarbanes-Oxley Act of 2002 (SOX)*** (180 days). Protects employees of certain companies who report alleged mail, wire, bank or securities fraud; violations of the Securities and Exchange Commission (SEC) rules and regulations; or violations of Federal laws related to fraud against shareholders. The law covers employees of publicly traded companies and companies required to file certain reports with the SEC.

Consumer Safety Laws

- ***Consumer Product Safety Improvement Act (CPSIA)*** (180 days). Protects employees who report to their employer, the federal government, or a state attorney general reasonably perceived violations of any statute or regulation within the jurisdiction of the Consumer Product Safety Commission (CPSC). CPSIA covers employees of consumer product manufacturers, importers, distributors, retailers, and private labelers.

- ***FDA Food Safety Modernization Act (FSMA)*** (180 days). Protects employees of food manufacturers, distributors, packers, and transporters for reporting a violation of the *Food, Drug, and Cosmetic Act,* or a regulation promulgated under this law. Employees are also protected from retaliation for refusing to participate in a practice that violates this law.

If you believe that you have been retaliated against, call 1-800-321-OSHA (6742) to be connected to the nearest OSHA office to report your complaint. For more information, visit OSHA's Whistleblower page at www.whistleblowers.gov.

Workers' Rights

Under OSHA law, workers are entitled to working conditions that do not pose a risk of serious harm. To help assure a safe and healthful workplace, the law provides workers with the right to:

- File a confidential complaint with OSHA to have their workplace inspected.
- Receive information and training about hazards, methods to prevent harm, and the OSHA standards that apply to their workplace. The training must be done in a language and vocabulary workers can understand.
- Receive copies of records of work-related injuries and illnesses that occur in their workplace.
- Receive copies of the results from tests and monitoring done to find and measure hazards in their workplace.
- Receive copies of their workplace medical records.
- Participate in an OSHA inspection and speak in private with the inspector.
- File a complaint with OSHA if they have been retaliated against by their employer as the result of requesting an inspection or using any of their other rights under the OSH Act.
- File a complaint if punished or retaliated against for acting as a "whistleblower" under the 21 additional federal laws for which OSHA has jurisdiction.

For more information, visit OSHA's Workers' Rights page at www.osha.gov/workers.html.

OSHA

OSHA has a great deal of information to assist employers in complying with their responsibilities under OSHA law. Several OSHA programs and services can help employers identify and correct job hazards, as well as improve their injury and illness prevention program.

Establishing an Injury and Illness Prevention Program

The key to a safe and healthful work environment is a comprehensive injury and illness prevention program.

Injury and illness prevention programs are systems that can substantially reduce the number and severity of workplace injuries and illnesses, while reducing costs to employers. Thousands of employers across the United States already manage safety using injury and illness prevention programs, and OSHA believes that all employers can and should do the same. Thirty-four states have requirements or voluntary guidelines for workplace injury and illness prevention programs. Most successful injury and illness prevention programs are based on a common set of key elements. These include management leadership, worker participation, hazard identification, hazard prevention and control, education and training, and program evaluation and improvement. Visit OSHA's Injury and Illness Prevention Programs web page at www.osha.gov/dsg/topics/safetyhealth for more information.

Compliance Assistance Specialists

OSHA has compliance assistance specialists throughout the nation located in most OSHA offices. Compliance assistance specialists can provide information to employers and workers about OSHA standards, short educational programs on specific hazards or OSHA rights and responsibilities, and information on additional compliance assistance resources. For more details, visit www.osha.gov/dcsp/compliance_ assistance/cas.html or call 1-800-321-OSHA (6742) to contact your local OSHA office.

Free On-site Safety and Health Consultation Services for Small Business

OSHA's On-site Consultation Program offers free and confidential advice to small and medium-sized businesses in all states across the country, with priority given to high-hazard worksites. Each year, responding to requests from small employers looking to create or improve their safety and health management programs, OSHA's On-site Consultation Program conducts over 29,000 visits to small business worksites covering over 1.5 million workers across the nation.

On-site consultation services are separate from enforcement and do not result in penalties or citations. Consultants from state agencies or universities work with employers to identify workplace hazards, provide advice on compliance with OSHA standards, and assist in establishing safety and health management programs.

For more information, to find the local On-site Consultation office in your state, or to request a brochure on consultation services, visit www.osha. gov/consultation, or call 1-800-321-OSHA (6742).

Under the consultation program, certain exemplary employers may request participation in OSHA's **Safety and Health Achievement Recognition Program (SHARP)**. Eligibility for participation includes, but is not limited to, receiving a full-service, comprehensive consultation visit, correcting all identified hazards and developing an effective safety and health management program. Worksites that receive SHARP recognition are exempt from programmed inspections during the period that the SHARP certification is valid.

Cooperative Programs

OSHA offers cooperative programs under which businesses, labor groups and other organizations can work cooperatively with OSHA. To find out more about any of the following programs, visit www.osha.gov/dcsp/compliance_assistance/index_programs.html.

Strategic Partnerships and Alliances

The OSHA Strategic Partnerships (OSP) provide the opportunity for OSHA to partner with employers, workers, professional or trade associations, labor organizations, and/or other interested stakeholders. OSHA Partnerships are formalized through unique agreements designed to encourage, assist, and recognize partner efforts to eliminate serious hazards and achieve model workplace safety and health practices. Through the Alliance Program, OSHA works with groups committed to worker safety and health to prevent workplace fatalities, injuries and illnesses by developing compliance assistance tools and resources to share with workers and employers, and educate workers and employers about their rights and responsibilities.

Voluntary Protection Programs (VPP)

The VPP recognize employers and workers in private industry and federal agencies who have implemented effective safety and health management programs and maintain injury and illness rates below the national average for their respective industries. In VPP, management, labor, and OSHA work cooperatively and proactively to prevent fatalities, injuries, and illnesses through a system focused on: hazard prevention and control, worksite analysis, training, and management commitment and worker involvement.

Occupational Safety and Health Training

The OSHA Training Institute in Arlington Heights, Illinois, provides basic and advanced training and education in safety and health for federal and state compliance officers, state consultants, other federal agency personnel and private sector employers, workers, and their representatives. In addition, 27 OSHA Training Institute Education Centers at 42 locations throughout the United States deliver courses on OSHA standards and occupational safety and health issues to thousands of students a year.

For more information on training, contact the OSHA Directorate of Training and Education, 2020 Arlington Heights Road, Arlington Heights, IL 60005; call 1-847-297-4810; or visit www.osha.gov/otiec.

OSHA Educational Materials

OSHA has many types of educational materials in English, Spanish, Vietnamese and other languages available in print or online. These include:

- Brochures/booklets that cover a wide variety of job hazards and other topics;
- Fact Sheets, which contain basic background information on safety and health hazards;
- Guidance documents that provide detailed examinations of specific safety and health issues;
- Online Safety and Health Topics pages;
- Posters;
- Small, laminated QuickCards™ that provide brief safety and health information; and
- *QuickTakes*, OSHA's free, twice-monthly online newsletter with the latest news about OSHA initiatives and products to assist employers and workers in finding and preventing workplace hazards. To sign up for *QuickTakes* visit www.osha.gov/quicktakes.

To view materials available online or for a listing of free publications, visit www.osha.gov/publications. You can also call 1-800-321-OSHA (6742) to order publications.

OSHA's website also has a variety of eTools. These include utilities such as expert advisors, electronic compliance assistance, videos and other information for employers and workers. To learn more about OSHA's safety and health tools online, visit www.osha.gov.

OSHA Advisory Committees

OSHA sponsors advisory committees to advise the Secretary of Labor and the Assistant Secretary of Labor for Occupational Safety and Health on workplace safety and health issues.

All of OSHA's advisory committees have membership balanced between representatives of workers and employers, and most also include other qualified individuals such as government officials, safety and health professionals and members of the public. All committees accept comments from interested individuals. Transcripts and minutes of the meetings are also available to the public on the committee web pages at www.osha.gov/osha-advisory-committee.html.

The five current advisory committees are:

- The National Advisory Committee on Occupational Safety and Health (NACOSH), which advises, consults with and makes recommendations to the U.S. Secretaries of Labor and Health and Human Services (HHS) on matters regarding the OSH Act;
- The Advisory Committee on Construction Safety and Health (ACCSH), which advises the Secretary of Labor on construction safety and health standards and other matters;
- The Federal Advisory Council on Occupational Safety and Health (FACOSH), which advises the Secretary of Labor on all aspects of federal agency safety and health;
- The Maritime Advisory Committee for Occupational Safety and Health (MACOSH), which advises the Secretary of Labor on workplace safety and health programs, policies and standards in the maritime industry; and
- The Whistleblower Protection Advisory Committee (WPAC), which advises, consults with and makes recommendations to the Secretary of Labor on ways to improve the fairness, efficiency, effectiveness, and transparency of OSHA's administration of whistleblower protections.

In addition, OSHA may form short-term advisory committees to advise the agency on specific issues.

OSHA

NIOSH Health Hazard Evaluation Program
Getting Help with Health Hazards

The National Institute for Occupational Safety and Health (NIOSH) is a federal agency that conducts scientific and medical research on workers' safety and health. At no cost to employers or workers, NIOSH can help identify health hazards and recommend ways to reduce or eliminate those hazards in the workplace through its Health Hazard Evaluation (HHE) Program.

Workers, union representatives and employers can request a NIOSH HHE. An HHE is often requested when there is a higher than expected rate of a disease or injury in a group of workers. These situations may be the result of an unknown cause, a new hazard, or a mixture of sources. To request a NIOSH Health Hazard Evaluation go to www.cdc.gov/niosh/hhe/request.html. To find out more about the Health Hazard Evaluation Program:

- Call (513) 841-4382, or to talk to a staff member in Spanish, call (513) 841-4439; or
- Send an email to HHERequestHelp@cdc.gov.

OSHA

OSHA Regional Offices

Region I
Boston Regional Office
(CT*, ME, MA, NH, RI, VT*)
JFK Federal Building, Room E340
Boston, MA 02203
(617) 565-9860 (617) 565-9827 Fax

Region II
New York Regional Office
(NJ*, NY*, PR*, VI*)
201 Varick Street, Room 670
New York, NY 10014
(212) 337-2378 (212) 337-2371 Fax

Region III
Philadelphia Regional Office
(DE, DC, MD*, PA, VA*, WV)
The Curtis Center
170 S. Independence Mall West
Suite 740 West
Philadelphia, PA 19106-3309
(215) 861-4900 (215) 861-4904 Fax

Region IV
Atlanta Regional Office
(AL, FL, GA, KY*, MS, NC*, SC*, TN*)
61 Forsyth Street, SW, Room 6T50
Atlanta, GA 30303
(678) 237-0400 (678) 237-0447 Fax

Region V
Chicago Regional Office
(IL*, IN*, MI*, MN*, OH, WI)
230 South Dearborn Street
Room 3244
Chicago, IL 60604
(312) 353-2220 (312) 353-7774 Fax

Region VI
Dallas Regional Office
(AR, LA, NM*, OK, TX)
525 Griffin Street, Room 602
Dallas, TX 75202
(972) 850-4145 (972) 850-4149 Fax
(972) 850-4150 FSO Fax

OSHA

Region VII
Kansas City Regional Office
(IA*, KS, MO, NE)
Two Pershing Square Building
2300 Main Street, Suite 1010
Kansas City, MO 64108-2416
(816) 283-8745 (816) 283-0547 Fax

Region VIII
Denver Regional Office
(CO, MT, ND, SD, UT*, WY*)
Cesar Chavez Memorial Building
1244 Speer Boulevard, Suite 551
Denver, CO 80204
(720) 264-6550 (720) 264-6585 Fax

Region IX
San Francisco Regional Office
(AZ*, CA*, HI*, NV*, and American Samoa,
Guam and the Northern Mariana Islands)
90 7th Street, Suite 18100
San Francisco, CA 94103
(415) 625-2547 (415) 625-2534 Fax

Region X
Seattle Regional Office
(AK*, ID, OR*, WA*)
300 Fifth Avenue, Suite 1280
Seattle, WA 98104
(206) 757-6700 (206) 757-6705 Fax

*These states and territories operate their own
OSHA-approved job safety and health plans and
cover state and local government employees as
well as private sector employees. The Connecticut,
Illinois, New Jersey, New York and Virgin Islands
programs cover public employees only. (Private
sector workers in these states are covered by
Federal OSHA). States with approved programs
must have standards that are identical to, or at least
as effective as, the Federal OSHA standards.

Note: To get contact information for OSHA area
offices, OSHA-approved state plans and OSHA
consultation projects, please visit us online at
www.osha.gov or call us at 1-800-321-OSHA (6742).

How to Contact OSHA

For questions or to get information or advice, to report an emergency, report a fatality or catastrophe, order publications, sign up for OSHA's e-newsletter *QuickTakes*, or to file a confidential complaint, contact your nearest OSHA office, visit www.osha.gov or call OSHA at 1-800-321-OSHA (6742), TTY 1-877-889-5627.

For assistance, contact us.

We are OSHA. We can help.